UPDOG

US MILITARY BRANCHES

THE US NATIONAL GUARD IN ACTION

Marie-Therese Miller

Lerner Publications ◆ Minneapolis

To John, Harold, Warren, and my family members and friends who have served in the US military
With gratitude to all National Guard personnel

Lerner Publications Company
An imprint of Lerner Publishing Group, Inc.
241 First Avenue North
Minneapolis, MN 55401 USA

For reading levels and more information, look up this title at www.lernerbooks.com.

Main body text set in ITC Franklin Gothic Std.
Typeface provided by Adobe Systems.

Editor: Lauren Foley **Designer:** Mary Ross

Library of Congress Cataloging-in-Publication Data

Names: Miller, Marie-Therese, author.
Title: The US National Guard in action / Marie-Therese Miller.
Description: Minneapolis, MN: Lerner Publications, [2023] | Series: US military branches (Updog books) | Includes bibliographical references and index. | Audience: Ages 8–11 | Audience: Grades 2–3 | Summary: "The US National Guard aids communities during state and national emergencies. Discover the history of the National Guard, the work they do, and the tech they use" —Provided by publisher.
Identifiers: LCCN 2021047162 (print) | LCCN 2021047163 (ebook) | ISBN 9781728458311 (library binding) | ISBN 9781728463629 (paperback) | ISBN 9781728462523 (ebook)
Subjects: LCSH: United States—National Guard—Juvenile literature.
Classification: LCC UA42 .M553 2023 (print) | LCC UA42 (ebook) | DDC 355.3/70973—dc23

LC record available at https://lccn.loc.gov/2021047162
LC ebook record available at https://lccn.loc.gov/2021047163

Manufactured in the United States of America
1-50860-50197-1/27/2022

TABLE OF CONTENTS

ALWAYS READY, ALWAYS THERE

A disease was spreading.

The National Guard brought medical supplies to hospitals. They helped test people for the disease.

The National Guard began as militias in Massachusetts in 1636. A 1916 law gave it more national duties.

MILITIA: a group of community members who train for the military

It has two parts, the Army National Guard and the Air National Guard.

UP NEXT!

National Guard jobs.

NATIONAL GUARD MISSION

National Guard members serve their state and the US.

They help during natural disasters like blizzards. They also fight in wars.

NATURAL DISASTER:
an event, such as a fire or flood, that could hurt many people

Most National Guard members serve part time.

They train one weekend each month and two weeks every year. They also work regular jobs.

PART TIME: working only some of the time

VEHICLE CLOSE-UP

The KC-135 Stratotanker refuels other aircraft in flight. Then the other aircraft can fly farther without landing.

AIRCRAFT:
any vehicle that flies

engines
boom

Some National Guard members are in the Army Special Forces. They are called Green Berets.

They work in small teams. They leap from aircraft and dive underwater.

UP NEXT!

Air National Guard aircraft.

COOL PLANES!

The Air National Guard flies the KC-135 Stratotanker.

It can carry 200,000 pounds (90,719 kg) of extra fuel.

The C-17 Globemaster III is 174 feet long (53 m). It can carry big army vehicles like tanks.

It has a large door in the back to drop supplies from the air.

In 2021, there were nearly 450,000 National Guard members. They help keep people safe.

MILITARY MISSION

THE NATIONAL GUARD HAS TO MOVE VEHICLES ACROSS THE OCEAN. WHAT SHOULD THEY USE TO MOVE THEM?

A. A team of Green Berets

B. A C-17 Globemaster III

C. A K-135 Stratotanker

Answer: B

GLOSSARY

aircraft: any vehicle that flies

militia: a group of community members who train for the military

natural disaster: an event, such as a fire or flood, that could hurt many people

part time: working only some of the time

CHECK IT OUT!

Army
https://kids.britannica.com/kids/article/army/352785

Miller, Marie-Therese. *The US Coast Guard in Action*. Minneapolis: Lerner Publications, 2023.

Miller, Marie-Therese. *The US Navy in Action*. Minneapolis: Lerner Publications, 2023.

Morey, Allan. *U.S. National Guard*. Minneapolis: Pogo Books, 2021.

United States National Guard Facts for Kids
https://kids.kiddle.co/United_States_National_Guard

US Government: United States Armed Forces
https://www.ducksters.com/history/us_government/united_states_armed_forces.php

INDEX

PHOTO ACKNOWLEDGMENTS

Image credits: Tech. Sgt. Michael Matkin/US Air National Guard, pp. 4, 8; Sgt. Ryan Tatum/181st Infantry Brigade/US Army, p. 5; US Air Force, p. 6; Civ. Zac Lehr/US Army National Guard, p. 7; Master Sgt. Cheran Cambridge/US National Guard, p. 9; US Army, p. 10; Airman 1st Class Tiffany DeNault/US Air Force, p. 11; Senior Airman Marcel Williams/US Air Force, pp. 12–13; Spc. Steven Young/US Army, pp. 14–15; Capt. Zach Anderson/US Air Force, pp. 16–17; Master Sgt. Matt Hecht/US Air National Guard, p. 18; Senior Master Sgt. George Thompson/US Air Force, p. 19; Sgt. Sebastian Rothwyn/US Army National Guard, p. 20. Design elements: Andrey_Kuzmin/Shutterstock.com, anyababii/Getty Images.

Cover: Sgt. 1st Class Peter Morrison/US National Guard.